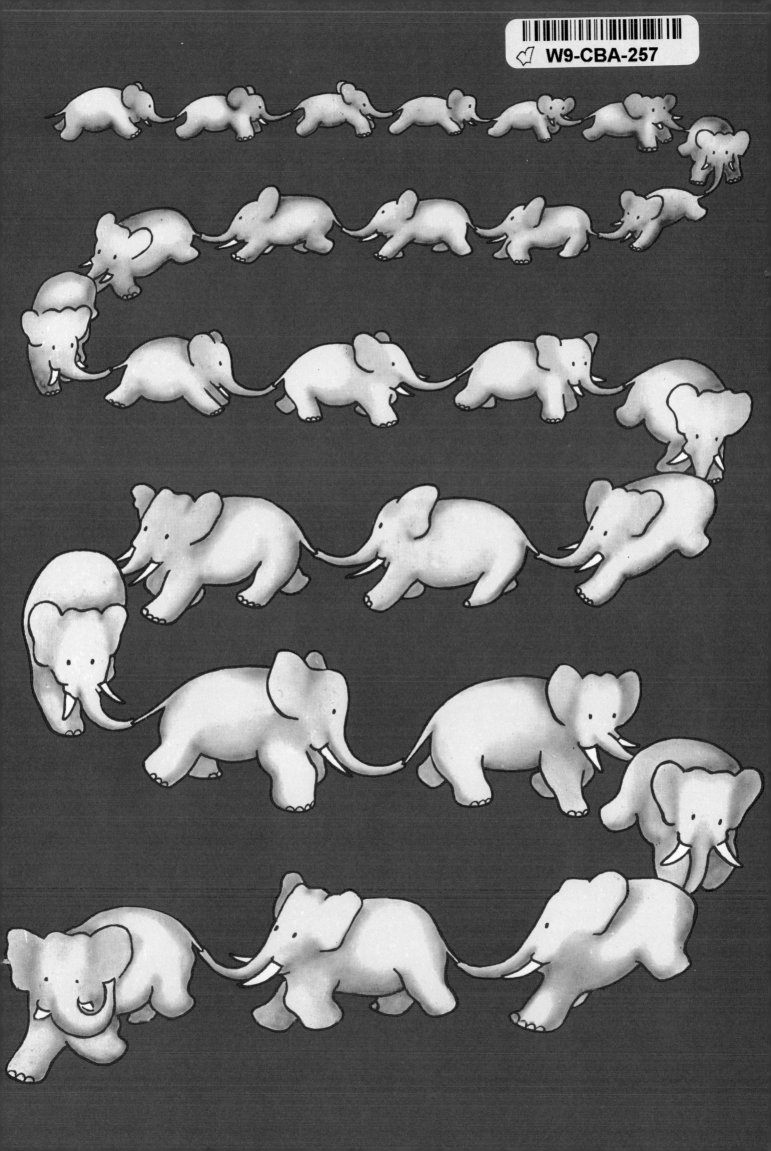

The Babar Books

The Story of Babar
The Travels of Babar
Babar the King
Babar and Zéphir
Babar and His Children
Babar and Father Christmas
Babar's Cousin: That Rascal Arthur
Babar's Fair
Babar and the Professor
Babar's Castle
Babar's French Lessons
Babar Comes to America
Babar's Spanish Lessons
Babar Loses His Crown
Babar's Trunk
Babar's Birthday Surprise
Babar Visits Another Planet
Meet Babar and His Family
Babar's Bookmobile
Barbar and the Wully-Wully
Babar Saves the Day
Babar's Mystery
Babar Learns to Cook
Babar the Magician
Babar's Little Library
Babar and the Ghost

The lovable little elephant who has endeared himself to children all over the world for more than a quarter of a century now gives his young American friends some French lessons.

And how delightful they are! Babar knows what boys and girls like, and so he has chosen to instruct them in those words and phrases that they are most likely to use from day to day.

To make the lessons easier, the French words are printed in blue, while the English translations of those words stand out in bold-face type.

LAURENT DE BRUNHOFF

BABAR'S

FRENCH LESSONS

LES LEÇONS DE FRANÇAIS DE

BABAR

RANDOM HOUSE New York

© Copyright, 1963, by Random House, Inc.

All rights reserved under International and Pan-American Copyright Conventions. Published in New York by Random House, Inc., and simultaneously in Toronto, Canada, by Random House of Canada, Limited. Manufactured in the United States of America.

This title was originally cataloged by the Library of Congress as follows: Brunhoff, Laurent de, 1925– Babar's French lessons. Les leçons de français de Babar. New York, Random House, 1963. 14 [i. e. 28] p. col. illus. 32 cm. 1. Title. PZ10.3.B7674Babi 63–18288 ISBN: 0-394-80587-9

1 JE SUIS BABAR, ROI DES ELEPHANTS

I am Babar, king of the elephants. I am French and I want to give you French lessons. Would you like that? Very well. Soon you will be able to speak to me in French.

The picture shows you how I look. Now say with me:

My head is ma tête.

My ears are mes oreilles.

My nose is mon nez. I mean **my trunk** is ma trompe.

And **my eyes** are mes yeux.

Now you must learn what I wear. Isn't that a wonderful suit of a becoming color?

This is **my green suit,** mon costume vert.

It is **my favorite,** mon préféré.

You say **coat and trousers?** I say veste et pantalon.

I wear **a nice tie**—une jolie cravate—with **a pink shirt,** une chemise rose.

What else? **My crown and my shoes.** Ma couronne et mes chaussures.

That's enough for the first lesson!

2   TOUS LES MATINS JE PRENDS UNE DOUCHE

Every morning I take a shower. First **a cold shower**–une douche froide–because I remain sleepy otherwise.

Then **a warm shower**–une douche chaude.

I wash myself. Je me lave.

My skin is thick, so I have to use a big brush with the soap. **A brush** is une brosse. **Soap** is savon.

I rub my arms. Je frotte mes bras.

I rub my stomach. Je frotte mon ventre.

I rub my back. Je frotte mon dos.

I rub my left leg. Je frotte ma jambe gauche.

I rub my right leg. Je frotte ma jambe droite.

And while I rub myself, **I sing.** Je chante. Do you sing when you are under the shower? What you certainly don't do is to shower yourself with a trunk. Only elephants can do that!

Then I take **a large towel**—une grande serviette—and **I dry myself.** Je me sèche.

And **I put on my clothes.** Je m'habille.

Then I am ready. Alors je suis prêt.

And this is enough for your second lesson.

Breakfast is delicious.

What do you like **to eat**—manger—for breakfast?

I like to eat cereal, but my wife, queen Celeste, prefers **a slice of bread and butter**—une tartine de pain beurré, or **a slice of toast**—une tartine grillée.

We drink a cup of tea. Nous buvons une tasse de thé.

Here are **my children**—mes enfants: Pom, Flora, Alexander, and Cousin Arthur.

"Good morning, Daddy," they say. "Bonjour, Papa."

The children drink **hot chocolate**—du chocolat chaud. They all love **crescents**—des croissants. What

are these? Delicious rolls; the French bakers are noted for them.

Arthur is greedy. Arthur est gourmand. He puts **four pieces of sugar**—quatre morceaux de sucre—in his chocolate. Then he mixes it carefully with **a spoon** —une cuillère.

Pom is always hungry. Pom a toujours faim. When the crescents are all eaten, he asks for bread. He puts a lot of butter on it with **a knife**—un couteau— and he adds **jam**—de la confiture—or **honcy**—du micl.

These are quite a few words for a third lesson, but breakfast is very important, **isn't it?** N'est-ce pas?

4 LES ENFANTS VONT A L'ECOLE

The children are **going to school.**

One, two, three, four, five. Un, deux, trois, quatre, cinq. There are five children going to school.

Five pupils—cinq élèves—who meet five others: **six, seven, eight, nine, ten.** Six, sept, huit, neuf, dix.

There are ten pupils carrying **ten briefcases**—dix cartables—on the way to school.

The teacher, **the Old Lady**—la Vieille Dame—is a very good friend of mine. Her pupils love her very much.

"Well, children," she says, "pick up **your notebooks**—vos cahiers— and **your pens**—vos plumes.

"Be careful not to make **ink blots**—des taches d'encre. Ready? Copy down what **I read**—je lis: 'The rabbit eats carrots and...'

"Now children, **open your books**—ouvrez vos livres—to page 27, **please**—s'il vous plaît. Compare it with what you have written. Then take

your **pencils**—vos crayons—and correct **your mistakes**—vos fautes."

After that, **she writes on the blackboard**—elle écrit sur le tableau noir—with **a piece of chalk**—un morceau de craie.

I like to go for a walk in the garden. There are **flowers of all colors**—des fleurs de toutes les couleurs.

Red	**Yellow**	**Blue**	**Pink**
Rouge	Jaune	Bleu	Rose

Celeste comes along and gathers flowers to make **a bouquet**—un bouquet. (See, it is the same word in French and English.) She loves **the roses**—les roses. (Another word that is the same in both languages!)

Really, this is not a difficult lesson, is it?

But now let's see which **tools**—outils—I need for working in the garden.

With **a rake**—un râteau—I clean **the path** —l'allée. Into **the wheelbarrow**—la brouette —I put **the leaves**—les feuilles—which have fallen from **the trees**—les arbres.

I have **vegetables**—des légumes—and **fruits** —des fruits. (Another word that is the same. . . .)

See **the scarecrow**—l'épouvantail? It frightens away **the birds**—les oiseaux—that might eat the fruit and vegetables.

I myself made the scarecrow with a very old suit and a hat that Celeste did not want me to wear any more.

6 MA MAISON A TROIS ETAGES

My house has three floors.

From **the balcony of my room**—le balcon de ma chambre—I can see **the roofs**—les toits—of Celesteville down to the lake.

Most of the time I stay in **the library**—la bibliothèque. It is a quiet room and I like to leave **the window open**—la fenêtre ouverte. All **the walls**—les murs—are lined with **books**—des livres.

When I read, I sit in **an armchair**—un fauteuil. When I write I use **the chair**—la chaise—at **the table**—la table.

Every day after school, the children knock at **the door**—la porte. I say **"Come in."** "Entrez." Then the three of them rush in to kiss me. Flora goes to the balcony, Alexander sits down on **the rug**—le tapis—and Pom asks me what I'm doing.

Sometimes I still have to work at night, when my children are asleep (when you too are asleep), because being a king is a hard job. Then I like **the curtains closed**—les rideaux fermés—and **a fire**—un feu—burning **in the chimney**—dans la cheminée. And **I light my pipe**—j'allume ma pipe.

7 LA VIEILLE DAME FAIT LA CUISINE

The Old Lady is cooking.

She is going to make **a chocolate cake**—un gâteau au chocolat—the children's favorite.

On the kitchen table—sur la table de la cuisine—she puts these things:

½ pound chocolate	2 tablespoons of rice flour instead of
¼ pound sugar	**flour**—farine
¼ pound butter	¼ pound of **shredded almonds**—
6 **eggs**—6 oeufs	amandes pilées

While the Old Lady softens the chocolate, Celeste softens the butter and Flora carefully beats **the whites of the eggs**—les blancs d'oeufs—very stiff. The Old Lady mixes everything in **a big bowl**—un grand bol. Then she puts **the dough**—la pâte—in a rather flat **baking pan**—moule. She must leave it **in the oven**—dans le four—at a low heat for about 45 minutes.

But Pom can hardly wait. He gets **his plate and his fork**—son assiette et sa fourchette. He wants to be all prepared **to taste**—pour goûter—the delicious cake.

You may try **the recipe**—la recette—but do not eat **too large a piece**—un trop gros morceau.

I play with the children.

They like **to play soccer**—jouer au football.

Yes, I mean "football" because your game of soccer is what we call football and your game of football is what we call rugby.

Isn't that funny?

Arthur likes to be **the goal-keeper**—le gardien de but.

"Pom, **pass the ball!**"—"passe le ballon!" shouts Alexander.

But Pom won't pass. **He runs**—il court—and keeps the ball for himself. He kicks . . .

Arthur catches the ball. Arthur attrape le ballon. Good for you, Arthur!

But Alexander teasingly says: "Oh, Pom, you are so **clumsy**—maladroit. **Look at me.** Regarde-moi. **He kicks the ball.** Il donne un coup de pied dans le ballon. The ball rolls out of bounds.

"Missed!" "Raté!" "Ha! Ha! Ha!" and Pom laughs.

You see, it is amusing to play soccer. In France we are as fond of soccer as you are of football or baseball.

But let me ask you something. Who will teach me how to play baseball? We don't have baseball in France.

The bicycle ride.

Who wants to go for a bicycle ride **this afternoon**—cette après-midi?

Hurray! Bravo! We all want to go. And **right away**—tout de suite—we get ready.

"I'll inflate **the tires**—les pneus," says Arthur.

"I'll fix **the brakes**—les freins," says Zéphir.

"I'll put **a drop of oil on the chain**—une goutte d'huile sur la chaîne," says Pom.

"I'll make a shiny **handlebar**—guidon," says Alexander.

"I'll prepare the things for **the picnic**—le pique-nique," says Flora. What excitement!

Then we hop on to **the saddle**—la selle—**and we pedal**—et nous pédalons.

Pom and Alexander race. Pom et Alexandre font la course.

"Let me go first!" shouts Alexander. But **he skids**—il dérape—**and falls down**—et tombe.

Poor Alexander! **He cries.** Il pleure, even though only his pants **are torn**—sont déchirés.

"Cheer up, Alexander," says Zéphir. **"Let's stop here**—arrêtons-nous ici—and start on the sandwiches."

Happy **birthday.** Today, **April twelfth**—le douze Avril—is **a great day**—un grand jour—for the Babars. It is Pom's birthday, and Flora's birthday, and Alexander's, because the three of them were born on the very same day.

They have invited all their friends. Ils ont invités tous leurs amis. Celeste has prepared **ice-cream**–de la glace–**cookies**–des biscuits–**candy and lollipops**–des bonbons et des sucettes, lots of **pineapple juice,** jus d'ananas, and a soft drink the children like very much: pink elephant punch.

Pom, Flora and Alexander were so happy with **their presents**–leurs cadeaux–that they kept on their new costumes. Pom feels very daring in his cowboy suit. "Nobody can beat me with **a gun**– un pistolet," he says to his admiring friend Catherine.

Flora has received exactly what she wished for: **a nurse's uniform**–un uniforme d'infirmière. As for Alexander, he is already telling of his adventures as a space elephant. Later on, Celeste organizes **games**–des jeux–and Pom's red cowboy **handkerchief**–mouchoir–is very useful for playing **Blindman's Buff**–Colin Maillard.

11 MA VOITURE VA VITE

My car is fast.

It is a good car with nice lines and a strong **motor**–moteur. We like it very much and Flora gave it a name—Josephine.

I need a car with **plenty of room**–beaucoup de place–because when I go riding I like to take along the whole family, as well as the Old Lady and Zéphir. That's a lot of people, and only two of them are thin . . .

Today we are going **on vacation**–en vacances.

Arthur has helped me to put **the luggage in the trunk**–les bagages dans le coffre. I push

the starter—le démarreur—and the motor roars. Arthur reminds me to stop at the service station to get **some gas**-de l'essence.

The man washes **the windshield**—le pare-brise. Then off we go . . .

I drive—je conduis—slowly while we're still **in town**—dans la ville. But as soon as we're away from crowds and **the highway is straight and empty**—l'auto route est droite et vide—Alexander shouts, **"Faster! Plus vite!** Go **at full speed!**-à toute vitesse!" And I drive a little faster.

We are going to the seashore.

We are going to swim and to dive. Nous allons nager et plonger. **There is the beach.** Voilà la plage.

Pom, Flora and Alexander run **on the sand**—sur le sable. They rush **into the waves**—dans les vagues. Hop!

Arthur has a spear and **goes fishing**—va à la pêche. He disappears for hours **in the water**—dans l'eau.

Have you ever gone swimming wearing goggles so you could see **the fish and the rocks**—les poissons et les rochers—underwater?

Zéphir prefers **to dig a hole**—creuser un trou—in the sand. Where is he? He is hiding in the hole!

The three little ones are making **a castle**—un château. They hope it will stand even when **the tide**—la marée—comes in. Flora decorates the castle with **shells and little pebbles**—des coquillages et des petits cailloux.

She is a real artist!

The Old Lady likes to rest under **the beach umbrella**—le parasol.

And I go out with Celeste in **my sailboat**—mon bateau à voile.

This is the best vacation in the world.

13 BEAU TEMPS ET MAUVAIS TEMPS

Good weather and bad weather.

Yesterday—hier—was a fine day and we could say: **"The sun is shining.** Le soleil brille.**"** Yesterday we needed **sunglasses**—des lunettes de soleil—and **straw hats**—des chapeaux de paille.

But **today it is raining**—aujourd'hui il pleut. I hope **the rain**—la pluie—will stop **tomorrow**—demain. We can see **the drops**—les gouttes—dripping down on the window pane. Drip, drip, drip!

It is impossible **to go out**—sortir—without **an umbrella**—un parapluie—or a rain hat and raincoat and **boots**—des bottes. Tell me, when you see **puddles**—des flaques—do you like to jump into them? That's not very nice. But Alexander does it and Flora cries when she is splashed with **mud**—la boue.

I don't like rain, but I love **snow**—la neige.

It is such fun to throw **snowballs**—des boules de neige, to build **a snow man**—un bonhomme de neige, and **to go skiing**—faire du ski. Or just stare at **the snowflakes**—les flocons de neige.

My bed is comfortable.

When **I am tired**—je suis fatigué—at the end of the day it is good **to go to bed**—se coucher.

I take off **my robe**—ma robe de chambre—and **my slippers**—mes pantoufles—and make sure I have **a glass of water**—un verre d'eau —near me.

I pull **the blanket**—la couverture—up to my neck.

Usually **I fall asleep very quickly**—je m'endors très vite.

Do you have **nice dreams**—des jolis rêves? I do. But sometimes I have **nightmares**—des cauchemars. Then **I wake up suddenly**— je me réveille brusquement.

Now, my friends, **I am very sleepy**—j'ai très sommeil. **I turn out the light**—j'éteins la lumière.

Good night. Bonne nuit. And **thank you** — merci — for having learned your French lessons so well.